Under My Feet

Rabbits

Patricia Whitehouse

Raintree

www.raintreepublishers.co.uk
Visit our website to find out more information about **Raintree** books.

To order:
☎ Phone 44 (0) 1865 888112
📠 Send a fax to 44 (0) 1865 314091
💻 Visit the Raintree Bookshop at **www.raintreepublishers.co.uk** to browse our catalogue and order online.

First published in Great Britain by Raintree, Halley Court, Jordan Hill, Oxford OX2 8EJ, part of Harcourt Education.
Raintree is a registered trademark of Harcourt Education Ltd.

Editorial: Diyan Leake and Kate Buckingham
Design: Sue Emerson and Michelle Lisseter
Picture Research: Jennifer Gillis
Production: Jonathan Smith

Originated by Dot Gradations
Printed and bound in China by South China Printing Company

ISBN 1 844 43732 9
08 07 06 05 04
10 9 8 7 6 5 4 3 2 1

British Library Cataloguing in Publication Data
Whitehouse, Patricia
Rabbits
599.3'2
A full catalogue record for this book is available from the British Library.

Acknowledgements
The publishers would like to thank the following for permission to reproduce photographs: Ardea London Ltd. pp. 5, 9; Bruce Coleman Inc. p. 13, 23 (David C. Reniz); Getty Images/Stone p. 18; Naturepl.com p.21 (Simon King); NHPA p.7 (Michael Leach); Oxford Scientific Films pp. 8, 10, 12, 14, 16, 17, 15, 19, 23 (Maurice Tibbs), 20 (Des & Jen Barlett); Photodisc p.4; Photo Researchers Ltd. p. 6, 11, 23 (Ernest Janes); Tudor Photography p. 23; Illustration on page 22 by Will Hobbs.

Cover photograph reproduced with permission of Ardea London Ltd./Ian Beames.

Every effort has been made to contact copyright holders of any material reproduced in this book. Any omissions will be rectified in subsequent printings if notice is given to the publishers.

Some words are shown in bold, **like this.**
You can find them in the glossary on page 23.

Contents

Do rabbits live here?. 4

What are rabbits? 6

What do rabbits look like?. 8

Where do rabbits live?. 10

What do rabbit homes look like?. . . . 12

How do rabbits find their way? 14

How do rabbits make their homes? . . 16

What is special about rabbit homes? . 18

When do rabbits come out
    from underground?. 20

Rabbit home map 22

Glossary 23

Index 24

Do rabbits live here?

Have you ever seen a rabbit?

When you go outside, you might be walking over one!

Some rabbits live under your feet.

Their homes are underground.

What are rabbits?

Rabbits are **mammals**.

All mammals have hair or fur on their bodies.

Mammals make milk for their babies.

These are young baby rabbits.

What do rabbits look like?

ear | tail | leg

Rabbits have long ears and big back legs.

Their tails are small and fluffy.

Most rabbits are brown or grey.

Some rabbits are about the same size as a cat.

Where do rabbits live?

Most rabbits do not live in a **hutch** or garden.

Some live underground.

These rabbits live together in a group called a **colony**.

Other rabbits live alone.

What do rabbit homes look like?

Rabbits live in **burrows**.

Burrows have **tunnels** and a **nest**.

Big burrows are called **warrens**.
Many rabbits live in a warren.

There are lots of tunnels and nests.

How do rabbits find their way?

Rabbits use their big ears to hear.

They can even hear sounds outside their **burrow**.

Rabbits use their noses to smell.

A mother rabbit can find her babies by their smell.

How do rabbits make their homes?

Rabbits use their paws to dig **tunnels** and **nests**.

They push the soil outside.

Rabbits put grass in their nests.

The grass keeps baby rabbits warm and dry.

What is special about rabbit homes?

Most **burrows** have many ways to get in and out.

This helps rabbits get away from danger quickly.

A mother rabbit keeps her babies safe.

When she goes to find food, she closes the hole to the **nest**.

When do rabbits come out from underground?

Rabbits come out of their **burrows** to eat.

Most rabbits eat in the morning and late afternoon.

Rabbits may leave their burrows if there is danger.

Most burrows have many ways to get out.

Rabbit home map

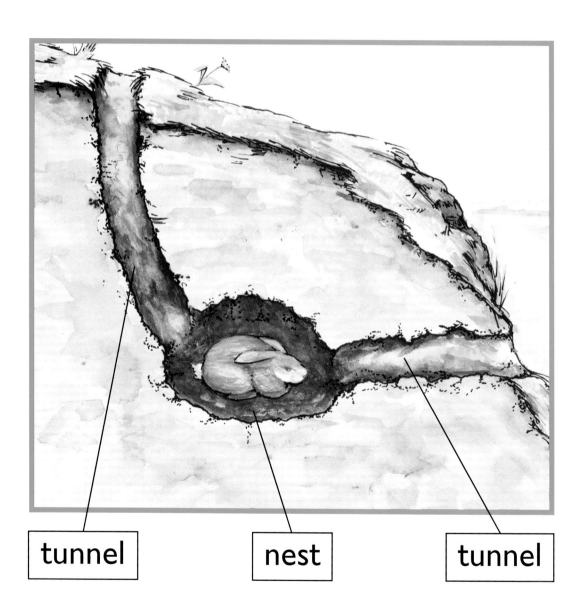

tunnel   nest   tunnel

Glossary

burrow
animal home underground

colony
group of rabbits that live together in the same burrow

hutch
home built for a pet rabbit

mammal
animal that has hair or fur and makes milk to feed its babies

nest
underground room where an animal may sleep, eat and look after its young

tunnel
hole underground

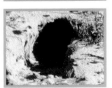
warren
big burrow with many tunnels and nests

Index

baby   7, 15, 17, 19

burrow   12, 13, 14, 18, 20, 21, 23

colony   11, 23

colour   9

danger   18, 21

ear   8, 14

food   19, 20

fur   6

hutch   10, 23

mammal   6, 7, 23

nest   12, 16, 17, 19, 22, 23

nose   15

paw   16

size   9

smell   15

tail   8

tunnel   12, 22, 23

warren   13, 23

 CAUTION: Remind children that it is not a good idea to handle animals.
Children should wash their hands with soap and water after they touch any animal.

Titles in the Under My Feet series include:

Hardback   1 844 43743 4

Hardback   1 844 43731 0

Hardback   1 844 43732 9

Hardback   1 844 43733 7

Find out about the other titles in this series on our website www.raintreepublishers.co.uk